Copyright © 20

All ri

ISBN: 1499141149
ISBN-13: 978-1499141146

# INTRODUCTION

I wrote this book as a service to those battling against DCPP. This book will not solve all of your problems. However, I hope that it will give you some insight into what lies in store for you or what you are currently going through. Keep in mind that nothing should be taken as legal advice and you should always defer to your lawyer.

You should also know a little about me. I am very different than any other lawyer you'll come across. While no one is right or wrong in the way they practice law, I have charted my own course. You see, most lawyers share common practices and beliefs. I however, go against the grain just as I have from as far as back as I can remember. Again, it's not to say I am better or that I know more, just that my take on things may be very different than most everyone else. Furthermore, I'm a bit of a cynic. Yes, there are some great people working for DCPP that are really helping families in need. These people don't get enough credit. Unfortunately, it seems like they are overshadowed by those that seek to harm families for their own benefit. I have seen too much to have faith in this organization as a whole. I approach DCPP as my enemy until and unless I am shown otherwise. Luckily, I have been shown otherwise and I have teamed up with DCPP to accomplish great things. Such encounters are far and few between however. Thus, everything you read here has been written with someone that has a slanted view so keep that in mind at all times.

This book is for reference purposes only. It is written for someone that is going through a DCPP case although it may be helpful to lawyers as well. However, it is not meant to be a legal treatise although I do cite to case law and statutes. Years ago, I probably wouldn't have bothered but I have noticed more and more clients attempting to educate themselves as to the law. Thus, I have included some basic principles in this book. I cannot include everything so you should not quote this book to your lawyer or anyone else as a legal authority. I have simplified many concepts and skipped over others. There reaches a point where too much law would be boring and confusing.

Finally, this book is not meant to be a commercial for my services or that of my firm. Of course, we would be more than happy to help you if you need us; however, it is not my intent to sell you on my services. Thus, I will sometimes discuss my view, my tactics and examples from my practice. I do this for a variety of reasons but selling you on my firm is certainly not one of them. I wish you the best of luck with your DCPP matter and I hope that you find this book valuable in your fight against DCPP.

# CONTENTS

|  | Acknowledgments | I |
|---|---|---|
| 1 | Understanding DCPP | 1 |
| 2 | Putting Your Emotions Aside | 7 |
| 3 | Hiring a Lawyer | 11 |
| 4 | How DCPP is Notified | 19 |
| 5 | DCPP Investigations | 29 |
| 6 | Investigative Findings | 41 |
| 7 | OAL Appeals | 51 |
| 8 | Order to Investigate | 57 |
| 9 | The Order to Show Cause | 61 |
| 10 | Compliance and Case Management | 67 |
| 11 | Fact Finding Hearing | 71 |
| 12 | Permanency Hearing | 79 |
| 13 | GM Hearings | 83 |
| 14 | FG Complaints | 87 |
| 15 | Termination of Parental Rights | 89 |
| 16 | Kinship-Legal Guardianship | 95 |

# ACKNOWLEDGMENTS

The author wishes to thank several people. I would like to thank all of my employees. I have put together a group of lawyers and administrative staff that work hard for the firm's clients. I am truly proud of them and the results that they achieve our clients. Speaking of which, I would also like to thank all of our clients. Thousands of people have entrusted us to take care of their most serious legal matters. Without them, there would be no firm. Finally, I would like to thank all my colleagues, friends and family that continue to offer their encouragement and support.

Special thanks goes to Morgan Rice, Esq. and Bonnie Jeanne Horwath who helped me edit this book.

# 1. UNDERSTANDING DCPP

I view all of my cases as a war and you should too. In order to win a war, you need to know your enemy. As I stated in my introduction, DCPP is not always your enemy. Sometimes it can be your greatest ally. Only an experienced lawyer can really help you determine if DCPP will be friend or foe. You should never make any assumptions about its intentions. I don't care how nice the case workers are to you. One of the 36 Stratagems from ancient China is to hide a knife behind a smile; that is, charm your enemy and then stab him after you've gained his trust.

The Division of Child Protection and Permanency is the agency formally known as DYFS (the Division of Youth and Family Services). The name change was just cosmetic; it is still the same agency. Most people associate DCPP with child abuse such as hitting children. However, most cases that I deal with do not involve physical abuse. For DCPP to be involved, all that is required is a risk of harm. This really throws off a lot of people as they don't understand the law. Thus, I will often hear people tell me how they didn't hit their kids and therefore, they did nothing wrong. This is one of many deadly assumptions that too many people make.

DCPP has a number of units within it and it's important that you understand at least three of the primary units. The first is the intake unit. Just as the name implies, it investigates new allegations and determines if a case should be closed or if it should proceed further. This also throws off a lot of people because they don't think that they 'have a case'. Trust me; if DCPP is talking to you, there is a case in the sense that there is a file in their office. You are being investigated. The only thing they don't know is whether the case will go to court. The term we use is litigation which is just a fancy word that indicates that a case of any type is in court. Thus, you may hear a case worker tell you that the case is 'going to litigation'.

If the case will move forward either in court or by providing services out of court, the case will be transferred to the permanency unit. This will be your long term case worker. If your parental rights are terminated, the case will be transferred to the adoption unit that will work to get the child adopted. It's important to understand these units and how a case flows through the office because it helps to explain at least some of DCPP's possible motivation. Look at it this way, if a case is not brought to court, there will not be much for the permanency unit to do. If your parental rights are never terminated, there is no need for an adoption unit. I'm sure you understand the precarious position the State economy is in and how the Government would love to slash budgets to save money. Thus, the jobs of many people literally depend on cases being dragged out and children being adopted out. If all of these people were just sitting around all day, I'm sure someone in Trenton would eliminate these positions. If they are always busy, they always have a job.

Of course, this is just my opinion. It clearly doesn't explain all of their actions and I doubt anyone associated with DCPP would ever admit that I am correct. Sometimes agencies like this suffer from group think. That is, the senior people that have been there for a while become jaded. They have seen the worst and they paint everyone with a broad brush. The new people that come in are indoctrinated with the same belief system. Independent thought is discouraged. Now this I have seen firsthand with a number of agencies. Thus, someone from DCPP may look at you like a scumbag that deserves to have their children taken away even though you did nothing wrong. But again, I cannot stress enough that I have met some awesome people that work for DCPP. Unfortunately, it is my view that they are in the minority.

You will likely deal with a number of people. If DCPP comes to your house for an emergency or after hours, you will likely be dealing with a SPRU worker. This person is on call 24/7 for a period of time so that emergency situations can be addressed. They likely won't remain on your case after the emergency dies down. The next person that comes out will be the intake worker. As I explained before, they will help determine where the case goes from there. Their boss is simply known as a supervisor. The supervisor's boss is the case work supervisor or case work *supe* (pronounced soup) for short. The person in charge of all of those people on the local level is the office manager. Each county has one or more DCPP offices. Larger counties have up to four while smaller counties just have one.

Besides the case workers and other people that work for DCPP, the agency also works very closely with a number of service providers. Some of these service providers are so good that I use them as well. Unfortunately, many are horrible. For example, I can send a client to 10 different people for a substance abuse evaluation and all 10 will say that my client doesn't have a problem. However, if you go to DCPP's evaluator, they will often say that you need some sort of drug treatment. From a cynic's point of view, this all seems too convenient to just be coincidence. Whether it is a conspiracy or just a mutual understanding is irrelevant. The bottom line is that DCPP's service providers should be approached with extreme caution. Only an experienced attorney can advise you if you should use their provider or an outside provider.

DCPP has their own lawyers but they don't work for DCPP directly. The Office of Attorney General otherwise known as the Attorney General's Office employs numerous lawyers known as Deputy Attorney Generals or DAGs for short. These DAGs represent a number of state agencies including DCPP. Think of the AG's office as a law firm. They are representing a client but they are not the client. This can sometimes present problems when a DAG must do what his client wants even though he may disagree personally. This differs from dealing with a prosecutor in a criminal case who usually has complete control over the case. As a defendant in a case, you may have no interaction with the DAG. Instead, your lawyer will work with him or her to resolve your matter one way or another. Like any other group of people, some are great, some aren't.

Another person that you will get to know if your case goes to court is the Law Guardian. This person represents the child (or children) when the case is in court. If the case has not reached court yet, there is no Law Guardian as one has to be appointed by the court. While the Law Guardian is a completely separate agency (actually an arm of the Public Defendant's office) they often work hand in hand with DCPP. Of course, there are some that are a non-entity in your case and there are others that can be your greatest ally. They have their own investigators that may come visit you at some point while the case is in court. Treat them just as you would anyone working with DCPP unless your lawyer advises otherwise.

Now that you have at least a basic understanding of the organization itself and who the players are, we can move on to discuss handling a DCPP case.

## 2. PUTTING YOUR EMOTIONS ASIDE

If you only get one thing out of this book, I hope it's this: You are your greatest enemy in a DCPP case. Your life was probably normal. Perhaps you've never been arrested before. If you've been to court, it's probably just for a traffic ticket. Your children are fine, and you don't beat them. Now all of a sudden your life is turned upside down with a knock on the door. Two DCPP workers and some police show up at your house late at night and they want to come in and tear your life apart. This is all based on an anonymous and/or bogus allegation. You've never done anything wrong and you are being treated like a criminal. You are scared, nervous, confused and probably very angry. In other words, you are very emotional.

When we think with our emotions, we are not thinking rationally. The best thing you can do is put your emotion aside and approach this entire situation from a calm and rational manner. Easier said than done, I know. Okay, seriously, this may seem impossible and for some people, it probably is. That is why I strongly urge everyone to hire a good lawyer right away (see next chapter). A lawyer approaches the case with a cold, calculating matter. I don't care if it's the right or wrong thing to do. I don't get emotionally involved. You are in a world of trouble and it's my job to get you out of it whether you actually did something wrong or not.

Realizing that it may be impossible to put your emotions completely aside, you at least have to calm down. Focus on getting DCPP out of your life before you focus on anything else. Do not focus on getting back at the person that made the allegations, finding out who made them, getting revenge on them, suing them, suing DCPP, etc. None of these things will help you win your case. Your sole focus should be getting out from under this case.

Besides thinking about the worst case scenario, you need to stop looking at the case with rose colored glasses. Out of all the phone calls I receive, the strangest by far has to be the people that call me to tell me how they don't need a lawyer. Clearly, these people want to stick their heads in the sand and think it will all go away. They need me to validate their false beliefs and of course, I won't do it. When that happens, they want to debate the situation with me.

I hear all sorts of excuses as to why someone doesn't need a lawyer. One of the most common is that the case worker was nice and said it wasn't a big deal. What these clients fail to realize is that some case workers lie. My firm has represented many hundreds of clients with DCPP matters. Almost every single one of them has reported that the case worker lied to them and/or to the court. Every single one of them cannot be wrong.

Look at it this way; do you think the fox is going to give you tips on guarding the hen house? Put another way, what would your reaction be if the case worker said 'we are looking to gather evidence against you so that we can take your kid away from you. We think you guys are scum bags and we know a nice foster family that is willing to adopt your kid. In order to gather evidence against you to accomplish this, we need you to sign consent forms, sign case plans, subject yourself to interviews and undergo various evaluations. After this is over, we will take you to court'. You'd probably lawyer up real quick huh?

But instead, if they say; 'hey, this is no big deal. We are looking to close out the case. We just need you to do this and that so we can close it out and go away'. The goal in both scenarios is the same; your cooperation. How do you think you would react to either scenario? (Of course, the case worker may be serious when they say they have every intention of closing the case right away. However, you may never know if they are telling the truth).

Your emotions don't cease becoming your enemy just because the case has gone to court and you now have a lawyer. A prolonged DCPP battle is very emotional, especially if you have limited to no access to your children. Even with a great attorney, it could take many months to even make a little bit of progress. Days seem like years. It seems like the case will never end and no matter what you do, it's never good enough for DCPP or the court. As a result, you wind up doing something stupid such as abusing substances. I have seen people accused of drug use who were innocent but because of the allegations, they actually started using. I have also seen clients stay clean for months only to get frustrated and start using again.

The best way to approach a DCPP case is to first calm down as much as possible. Find a good lawyer that will be your rock. Lean on him or her. Do not get into any fights with the case worker. Use your lawyer as the complaint department. Focus on ending the case, not getting back at DCPP or someone else. Admit the problems you have and put your pride aside. Focus on the fact that if you do not have your children, you will get them back at some point if you do the right thing. If you don't completely surrender to all of your problems and get all of the help that you need, there is a good chance that you will lose your children.

I hate to be morbid, but as I write this book, I recently had a client die after I worked so hard to get her child back. The case started with the father of the child overdosing. At this point, the child is still a baby and will never know her parents because they were too focused on drugs and not their child. Sadly, this is not the first client that died in such a matter and will certainly not be the last. Please don't emulate them. No matter what your problem is, focus on what is important and put everything else aside.

## 3. HIRING A LAWYER

Child Protective Services agencies across this country are waging a war against the poor, and DCPP in New Jersey is no different. If you are a lawyer and you want to make nice money, handling DCPP cases is probably the worst area of law to be in. The majority of people seeking your services will have no money. It's probably why not many lawyers specialize in this area; much less have any idea what they are even doing. For some of you, this chapter will be geared more towards convincing you to stick with the public defender than hiring a lawyer because a cheap lawyer can be very dangerous. As I indicated, this book is geared more towards people that don't have money for a lawyer but since some people have family members that eventually step up, I will address all aspects of hiring a lawyer.

Your first question will be whether or not you will hire a lawyer and when. With regard to the when, it should be right away. If you even hear someone mention the words DCPP, DYFS, CPS, police or anything else that gives you any indication that some agency may be contacting you to investigate an allegation of child abuse or neglect, you should hire a lawyer right away. Too many people think that they can go it alone, but this is like playing Russian roulette. Sure, you may come out fine, but when it doesn't, it could end very badly for you. Why gamble with your family like that?

Other people think that hiring a lawyer will make them look guilty and/or upset DCPP. Trust me; you cannot look guiltier than you already do. I have never seen someone hire a lawyer and as a result, their case got worse. It can only help you. As I have said before, you have no idea what you are doing and anything you say can be used against you. I'm sure you wouldn't perform surgery on yourself, so don't try to play lawyer.

Of course, this is all well and good if you can afford a lawyer and many people cannot. However, there is a big difference in cost between in court cases and out of court cases. Many people have no concept of what lawyers cost and trust me, all good lawyers are expensive. While you probably don't have enough money in your wallet to fully retain a lawyer for an out of court case, most people should be able to put together a short term payment arrangement to hire a lawyer. Some lawyers, such as me, also take credit cards. Out of court cases are cheaper because there are no court appearances which is where most of the legal work is done during an in court case. Furthermore, we are able to keep almost all of our out of court cases from going to court which saves our clients a lot of aggravation in addition to a lot of money. If you truly have no money, you cannot get a public defender for an out of court case. You can only get a public defender when your case goes to court.

You don't get a public defender just by asking for one; you also have to qualify. Thus, if you qualify for a public defender, you probably cannot afford a good lawyer in the first place. So, there really is no choice here; or at least there shouldn't be. Unfortunately, there are a growing number of lawyers that will take a case for next to nothing. In the vast majority of these situations, these lawyers are very bad and will cause a lot of damage to your case. Some may literally have no idea what they are doing. Trust me, I hear horror stories almost every day and I've seen a number of them in action. A little bit of common sense could have saved these people a lot of aggravation. Think about it this way, if these people charge 50% or even 20% of what I charge, why would anyone hire me? Are the thousands upon thousands of people that hire me just really stupid? Like anything else, you get what you pay for. If you hire a cheap lawyer, you will likely suffer the consequences.

The main reason why people hire cheap lawyers is because they can't afford a good lawyer in the first place but they think that their public defender will not do a good job. Like any other group of people, there are great public defenders and just as there are bad ones. In fact, I know some amazing public defenders that I bounce ideas off of because they have an incredible amount of knowledge and experience. Also keep in mind that not all public defenders work for the public defender's office. Many are 'pool attorneys'; private attorneys who contract with the public defender's office to take cases that the public defender cannot due to a conflict. These pool attorneys are not paid well at all. In fact, a good attorney can often make more in an hour than they will make in a day. Thus, some of these lawyers can be pretty bad. Of course, some are really great. For whatever reason, they just don't seek out the big money.

Public defenders of all types are underpaid and overworked. They have little incentive to offer great customer service. It's very difficult to fire them and their pay is not dependent upon your satisfaction. Thus, while they may be doing a good job on your case, your perception (which is reality to you) is that they are doing a horrible job. Compare this to a private attorney that you hire. If you don't like this attorney, you can fire him or her and hire someone else. Thus, there is great incentive to give you the best customer service possible. Likewise, you have chosen this attorney whereas you are stuck with whatever public defender you get.

It's worth repeating that the best thing to do is to hire the best lawyer you can as early as you can. Too many people wait to hire a good lawyer. They think (assume) that the case will be easy and therefore, they can get by without a good lawyer. Too many are proven dead wrong. Other people have family members that only decide to help after realizing that the case has spiraled out of control after many months of litigation. Whatever the case, these people will likely pay more in legal fees by getting a lawyer involved later. When you hire a lawyer at the beginning of the case, you are giving that person a clean slate to work with. When you wait, the prior lawyer has likely created a huge mess that the new lawyer needs to clean up. In addition, the lawyer has to get caught up on everything that has gone on up to that point. In order to know where you're going, you have to know where you're coming from. That involves reviewing the file and probably reviewing the audio CDs of several court appearances. This can be very time intensive and whenever you are dealing with lawyers, time is money. Thus, do yourself a favor and hire a good lawyer as soon as you can.

Finding a good DCPP lawyer can be difficult. First, there are only a few of us that actually know what we are doing while there are more that will yes you to death just to take your money. We have too many lawyers in New Jersey and the economy has been bad for years. Instead of referring these cases out, too many lawyers will take the case just to make a dollar. For all the lawyer jokes out there, clients generally trust lawyers. It's like going to a doctor. If you go to a podiatrist about your heart, the doctor will kick you out and send you to a cardiologist. Unfortunately, the same doesn't apply to lawyers. Lawyers can practice almost any area of law they want at any time. So, you have to separate out the all-stars from the pretenders.

The internet can be one of the best ways to find a good lawyer. However, don't just hire a lawyer because they came up first in your Google search. Some lawyers pay to be up that high either by buying Google ads or by paying another company to boost their organic search ratings. Furthermore, many firms hire companies to write their website content. Thus, the impressive content you see may be from a non-lawyer in another state that works for a website development company. Look for a lawyer with an actual track record of experience with DCPP matters. If you can't find that on the website, ask the lawyer how many DCPP cases they have had, what counties they have been in, what judges they have been in front of, how many cases they won, etc. Don't settle for general answers. Ask about their last few cases. When were they? What were the facts? What were the results? When was the last time they were in court for a DCPP case? It's harder to fake details like this.

Do not rely on family friends to help you. I have seen this for years and I think these lawyers are insane. I have had a number of family members who needed legal help outside of my practice areas. Instead of winging it, I referred them to other lawyers that practiced in that area. You don't want to be anyone's guinea pig. Instead, ask them if they know of any good DCPP lawyers. If not, see if they will help you search for one.

Another mistake people make is using a family law attorney for a DCPP matter when that person knows nothing about DCPP matters. Most family law attorneys handle divorce, child custody and child support matters. Most have little to no experience with DCPP matters. In my opinion, DCPP is a completely different area of practice although there is some cross over between family law and DCPP issues. Sometimes people seek out family law attorneys not realizing that there is such a difference. Other people go back to their divorce attorney because they have used them in the past or are using them now. Again, never assume your lawyer knows what he or she is doing even if they have done a good job for you in a previous case. You need to question this lawyer just as you would any other. Chances are, they are probably not the right lawyer for your case.

Whatever lawyer you choose, just remember that you are the boss. You make all the final decisions and the lawyer works for you. Expect to be able to communicate with your lawyer and fully understand everything about your case. What is expected of you? What is the plan for the case? Hiring a good lawyer is an investment in your future and the future of your family. Do whatever you can to hire the best lawyer possible but don't just hire a private lawyer for the sake of having a private lawyer. Cheap lawyers will likely cost you. You will almost always be better off with a public defender than a cheap lawyer. Whatever you do, do it as soon as possible. Waiting to see what is going to happen is never a plan or a strategy.

## 4. HOW DCPP IS NOTIFIED

DCPP has a toll free number that anyone can dial to make an anonymous referral. DCPP must follow up on every single referral. This leads to a number of concerns that some people may abuse the system by making repeated, false referrals. While this does happen occasionally, it is not as widespread as you may think. The assistance of an attorney can be very helpful in fighting off numerous referrals. You should not assume that since the last 2, 3, etc., number of referrals were closed out quickly that this new one will be closed out just as quickly. At some point, DCPP gets sick of dealing with you and they may really look to turn your life upside down.

Despite the hotline, most of my cases seem to come from identifiable sources. The most common sources of referrals include hospitals, doctors, therapists and other mental health professionals, schools and police. Referrals from these sources carry much greater weight than referrals from anonymous sources. These identifiable people can come to court and testify against you.

Thus, while every DCPP case is serious, extra attention needs to be given to cases involving identifiable referral sources.

There are a number of reasons why these identifiable sources report cases to DCPP to quickly and readily. One reason is the fear of law suits. Everyone is afraid that if they don't report something and the child is later harmed, someone will turn around and sue. This is in addition to the negative media exposure that they would also receive. Another reason is because the person or entity calling in the referral has some sort of affinity for DCPP. Some doctors and therapists actually have a DCPP contract where they do a lot of work for them in addition to their private clients. This is not always disclosed and as a result, you may be confessing drug use, mental health issues, physical abuse and other issues to someone that has a direct link to DCPP. Thus, you should be careful in what you disclose and to whom. Be sure to ask if the person you are meeting with has a contract with any state agencies and if they have ever had to report one of their patients to a state agency for any reason. If so, what was the reason?

Of course, the primary reason why these people or agencies report suspected abuse is that it is the law. Everyone is obligated to report the abuse immediately. N.J.S.A. 9:6-8.10, State v. Hill, 232 N.J. Super. 353, 356 (Law Div. 1989). DYFS must cooperate with law enforcement, and law enforcement must cooperate with the Division. New Jersey Div. of Youth and Family Services v. Robert

M., 347 N.J. Super. 44, 63 (App. Div.), certif. denied, 174 N.J. 39 (2002).

I am often asked about actions that a parent can take in response to a false allegation. A lot of these questions get asked before the allegation has been proved to be false. Thus, they are putting the cart before the horse. Regardless, there is often little that a parent can do in response to a false allegation because of the immunity granted to reporters.

The law states that 'anyone that makes reports under this act shall have immunity from any liability, civil or criminal, that might otherwise be incurred or imposed'. N.J.S.A. 9:6-8.13. Immunity to a reporter of child abuse is conditioned upon the reporter acting pursuant to N.J.S.A. 9:6-8.10, which provides: Any person having reasonable cause to believe that a child has been subjected to child abuse or acts of child abuse shall report the same immediately to the Division of Youth and Family Services by telephone or otherwise. In making a report 'pursuant to this act' a person must have 'reasonable cause to believe that a child has been subjected to child abuse or acts of child abuse'. While there is no legislative intent to protect those people who report child abuse without any reasonable ground for so doing, F.A. v. W.J.F., 248 N.J. Super. 484, 491 (App. Div. 1991), it will likely be extremely difficult to prove that reasonable grounds did not exist. Damages may also be speculative so it may be very difficult to find a lawyer willing to take the case at all and even more difficult to find a lawyer willing to take the case on a contingency basis.

## -The Law Enforcement Connection

DCPP is not a law enforcement agency. However, they routinely work with law enforcement in a variety of ways to get what they want. In fact, the law requires both groups to work together. N.J.S.A. 9:6-8.36(a) requires DCPP to report all instances of suspected child abuse and neglect to the county prosecutor of the county in which the child resides. N.J.A.C. 10:129-1.1(a) requires DCPP to refer to county prosecutors all cases that involve suspected criminal activity on the part of a child's parent, caretaker or any other person.

The court is required to forward to prosecutors a copy of any complaint alleging child abuse. N.J.S.A. 9:6- 8.25(a); N.J.S.A. 9:6-8.25(b); N.J.S.A. 9:6-8.10. Prosecutors are statutorily required to report to DYFS any complaint 'which amounts to child abuse or neglect'. The law even requires a specific institutional mechanism of cooperation encompassing investigational and adjudicatory phases as well. N.J. Div. of Youth and Family Serv's v. H.B., 375 N.J. Super. 148, 179 (App. Div. 2005). Therefore, you have DCPP, the Prosecutor's Office and the court all referring cases to each other.

This is important to understand for a number of reasons. DCPP may use the police to bully you around. When the case worker first comes to your house, they may bring the police with them. Unless they are doing a DODD removal, this is done only to scare the hell out of you, plain and simple. Not only do they bring the police but sometimes they can bring up to four officers. This seems like an incredible waste of resources, especially in smaller towns. We are conditioned to respect and cooperate with police. So while you may be hesitant to cooperate with the case worker, you will likely do whatever they want with a group of police officers staring at you. However, the police have no real power. Without a warrant, they cannot come in your house. You are under no duty to answer their questions. Failing to cooperate with the case worker is a different story. I'll discuss that more in the next chapter. The best thing you can do is to call a lawyer before you make any decision as to whether or not you will cooperate with the case worker.

Besides just being bullied, the DCPP-law enforcement connection can land you in jail. Anything you say to a case worker can and will be used against you, not only in a DCPP case, but also in a criminal prosecution. They do not have to read you any rights or tell you if they will notify law enforcement about what you have said. As I previously explained, the law requires them to work hand-in-hand with the prosecutor. Thus, you should assume that anything you say to a case worker you are also saying to a police officer.

While you don't have to be read your rights, you still have rights. This basic understanding of the Constitution is lost on many including case workers, lawyers and even judges! The thinking by most is that your right to remain silent only kicks in after you have been charged with a crime. Common sense would tell you that your rights would be pretty worthless at that point. Nevertheless, I've actually had to argue this point with judges who thought I was the crazy one. Luckily, there is some case law on my side. case of State v. P.Z., 152 N.J. 86 (1997) clearly indicates that the right to remain silent is not limited to criminal cases and investigations. Your right to remain silent attaches to any situation where statements can be used against you in a possible criminal prosecution, which includes DCPP cases.

While there are plenty of cases that indicate that you have the right to remain silent in civil cases and other contexts, this case specifically mentions DCPP investigations/cases. Of course, the case also indicates that you do so at your own peril since statements may be required to adequately complete certain services. If you fail to complete these services, you may not be able to restore your parental rights. This why you need a good lawyer to tell you when to talk and why. There is no way that you can determine whether invoking your right to remain silent may impact your parental rights and vice versa.

If you still don't believe that DCPP and police may be working together, consider these few examples. One client made a number of allegations against the mother of the child. DCPP got really upset with him for making these allegations and they turned the entire case around on him. The client spoke to the supervisor and she encouraged him to keep making the allegations. After they finished speaking, she told the case worker (out of my client's presence) that she wanted him to keep making these allegations because she was working with a detective. If he changed his story enough, she would get the detective to arrest him and charge him with a crime. Of course, they didn't know that my client was able to get a recording of this conversation and listen to it later.

In another case, my client was not permitted to be around the child who was living with the mother. The police followed the mother around and went to her house several times. They kept accusing her of having her husband in the house. I spoke to the detective and asked him why he would even care and what law was being broken. He said that no law would be violated but he knew that there was a court order in the DCPP case and that if he was at the house, the child would be removed. So yes, we have tax payer dollars paying the police to do DCPP's work. After I called, the stalking stopped.

In yet another case, my client was accused of molesting his daughter. However, he was never charged criminally because he was smart enough to call me before he said anything to the police. Nevertheless, I felt like there was a missing piece of the puzzle as something didn't add up. Nowhere in the DCPP file did it really explain exactly how the child made these disclosures. While I would seek to get the records of the Prosecutor's Office anyway, I really wanted to get them here. However, it took forever. Once I got them, I found out why.

When the child was first interviewed, she said that nothing happened. *'Daddy never did anything wrong.'* No matter what questions the detective asked, they kept hitting roadblocks. After the interview was over, the child apparently spoke to the mother (who was really against my client) and the case worker (who really had no business being there). Less than an hour later, the child was interviewed again and of course, she was full of allegations about all the bad things Daddy did to her. Conveniently absent from the interview is any questioning as to why the child would suddenly change her entire story and why it was done so quickly.

Keep in mind that the DCPP complaint only mentioned the second interview. I had no idea that the child had issues with disclosures or had been interviewed twice. It wasn't until I received the evidence from the prosecutor that I found out about all of this. Shortly thereafter, I filed a motion to dismiss the complaint. Without the need to even hire an expert, I argued that this was coaching and that there was no corroboration of the allegations. The motion to dismiss the complaint was granted.

Remember, it doesn't matter how innocent you are or how nice the case worker seems. You should assume the worst at all times. Too many people have assumed the best and suffered the consequences as a result. Don't be one of them. Even if you never speak to, see or even hear about law enforcement, do not assume that they are not actively working with DCPP to build a case against you.

## 5. DCPP INVESTIGATIONS

Nothing upsets me more than the improper handling of DCPP investigations by clients that think they know what they are doing. I have touched on this topic a few times already throughout this book. I get more calls about DCPP investigations than any other issue. There are three types of people that call. The first types are people that know they need a lawyer. Those are my favorite because the call goes very smoothly. The second types are people that are not sure. I try to be very clear that it is my opinion that everyone involved in any legal matter, especially a DCPP case, should have a lawyer. At the same time, I am not saying that they need to hire my firm.

The third types are people that believe that they don't need a lawyer. It seems like they are just calling me to convince themselves that they don't need a lawyer. It's a really strange phone call because no matter what I say, they have a reason as to why I'm wrong. When I try to talk some common sense to them, I sometimes get accused of scaring them into hiring me. This clearly ignores the fact that I don't beg for cases and I emphasize that I am not trying to get them to hire me, but that I think they should hire someone. Thus, this chapter will not only focus on DCPP investigations, but why I tell people that they should hire someone ASAP.

As previously mentioned, most DCPP investigations start with a referral. Regardless of who made the referral or what it is about, a case worker will need to talk to you. Occasionally, you will be told by someone that they or someone else has or will report you to DCPP. This is the time to hire a lawyer. You should not wait to see what happens. While it's not pocket change, it's not that expensive to hire a lawyer for a DCPP investigation.

In most cases, your first clue that there is a DCPP investigation is a knock on the door. This can happen anytime including nights and weekends. If it is after hours, the person knocking on your door will likely be a SPRU worker, which is an after-hours emergency worker. For safety and for added credibility, DCPP workers will often come in groups of two. There will be a primary worker and someone known as a 'buddy'. As I also indicated previously, the police may or may not accompany them.

This is most people's first encounter with DCPP or any legal situation for that matter. It comes as a complete shock and surprise. Your initial instinct is to comply and let them in the house. Before you know it, they have looked around your house, spoken to your children, spoken to you at length and probably convinced you to sign a bunch of documents. Depending on what you actually said or did, you may have really shot yourself in the foot already. Only once the stress and excitement of the event subsides do you hop on the Internet to find out what happened. It's then that you realize you made a huge mistake. To be clear, I am not giving you advice here or anywhere else in this book. Shutting the door in their face could lead to huge consequences including the removal of your children. This presents a real catch 22 situation: Do you comply and risk disaster or do you shut the door in their face and risk disaster? Without the assistance of an attorney to guide you, you are pretty much on your own. That's the reason why some lawyers (such as myself) make every effort to be available 24/7/365.

If you did shoot yourself in the foot by complying with them at first and then realize later that you need an attorney, don't beat yourself up over it. That's how most of my cases start and I have helped hundreds of people close the case without it going to court. Speaking of cases, don't let the word case throw you off. The DCPP worker will tell you that they are doing an investigation to see if they should open a case, that they haven't opened a case yet or that they need to talk to you so they can make sure that they don't have to open a case. However they say it, don't be fooled. If DCPP is talking to you, there was a referral and therefore there are documents that support that. These documents get placed in a file. They will make a finding at the end of the investigation and hold on to these documents and the result of the investigation for at least several years. Sure sounds like a case to me. No matter what you call it, this DCPP investigation is serious business and you should treat it as such no matter what the case worker says.

You wouldn't ask an inmate to set up the prison security system so why would you ever trust anything that the case worker says? Oh that's right; they were nice and said they wanted to close the case (or to not open a case depending on who your case worker is). What do you expect? If they came at you yelling and screaming and told you that you would likely have your children put in foster care next week, are you going to help them? Or would you be more willing to help them if they are nice to you and tell you that everything is going to be all right. Remember the saying, 'you catch more flies with honey'? Well you are the fly and DCPP knows what they are doing. You should view them as your biggest enemy.

To be clear, DCPP can and will lie to you. Again, I'm painting with a broad brush here. There are some great case workers as I have said before. I can't emphasize that enough. However, you have no capacity to judge whether or not the case worker is lying to you so don't even try to do it. Consider this: my firm has represented hundreds of people in every single court in New Jersey for DCPP matters. When you first get to court, you are served with a complaint which outlines all of the allegations against you. In almost every single case, my client has indicated that the complaint is filled with lies. Certainly, some of these clients might be lying to me but almost every single one of them? Quite often it's about issues which are mostly inconsequential so they would have little motivation to lie. It's so common that I warn my clients ahead of time so that they are not shocked. Despite that, most are still shocked. Thus, you need to assume that the case worker will do and say anything in order to take your children away. If you still need more convincing, read the last chapter again about the supervisor that tried to set up my client to get arrested by the police. They lied directly to his face and we had the evidence to prove it beyond a shadow of a doubt.

So when people ask me if they need an attorney, I often ask why they wouldn't get one. It just seems like common sense to me. You have nothing to lose except a small amount of money and everything in the world to gain. Now have people handled DCPP investigations by themselves and it turned out fine? Of course, plenty. But it's just like people playing Russian roulette with one bullet and a six shooter. Five people are going to walk away unscathed while one person will not be so lucky. Do you really want to take those odds?

Furthermore, don't ask the case worker if you should or can hire a lawyer. You won't like their answer, especially since it'll probably be something stupid like, 'well then we'll have to get our lawyers involved'. What's wrong with that? That's a good thing! Of course, it's said like it's a bad thing so it scares people into going without a lawyer.

Another common question I get is whether the hiring of a lawyer will upset DCPP and/or make it look like you are guilty. If you haven't caught on yet, they probably already think you are guilty; they just need the evidence to prove it. Regardless, I have never seen a case, whether it is DCPP, criminal, civil or anything else where the hiring of a lawyer results in negative consequences for the client. In fact, in almost every single case, it will lead to a positive outcome. Common sense should dictate that I am not going to get involved in a case if it is likely to cause a problem for you. Whenever I ask why they would even think that, the answer usually starts with 'I thought . . .' which is really just another way of saying 'I assumed . . .' and we all know what happens when we assume right?

If you still aren't sold on the fact that hiring a lawyer is the best thing to do in this situation, let me give you some numbers. As I have said, I have represented hundreds of clients in court and hundreds of clients out of court. The vast majority of my out of court clients never had to go to court. Some of the cases were shut down within just a few days; most in just a few weeks. The vast majority of my in court cases are the opposite. They did not have a lawyer help them during the investigation stage of the case. Instead, they shot themselves in the foot time and time again. Had they hired me, I probably could have kept the case out of court or at the very least, made the case much easier to deal with. Instead, they are spending more money and going through more stress. You just can't argue with this anecdotal evidence.

Despite all of that being said, some people will tell me how they are innocent and that they don't need a lawyer. Such a statement is beyond ridiculous. Regardless of how innocent or not they really are, some people have a defense mechanism where they look at everything with rose colored glasses because they don't want to even think about the worst case scenario. This inability to confront the worst case scenario may lead to disaster. I often tell them that they should watch the movie *Hurricane Carter* or look up *'the Innocence Project'*. While Hurricane Carter was one of the more famous people to go to prison, the Innocence Project has shown that many innocent people have been convicted and incarcerated for crimes they did not commit.

I understand you are not dealing with a criminal case so you may think none of this applies to you. However, think about it this way. A criminal case involves a prosecutor that may be much less biased than the lawyer representing DCPP. They have to first sell their case to the Grand Jury which may not be the hardest thing to do, but they still have to have their facts in order. They then have to worry about various motions the defense can file and a trial that might be years away. The burden of proof in a criminal trial is much higher than a DCPP case. Instead of one judge that might lean toward DCPP, the criminal case will be judged by jury and the prosecutor must get every single one of them to vote in his or her favor in order to secure a conviction. Thus, the prosecutor faces some long odds if they want to secure a conviction against someone who is actually innocent and yet, it has been proven that it has happened many times.

When you figure that DNA is not available in many cases to prove innocence or guilt, you have to realize that there are thousands upon thousands of people sitting in prison right now that are 100% innocent. So, when you claim that your DCPP investigation will be easy because you are innocent, you may want to reconsider since DCPP will have an easier road ahead than the prosecutor.

Finding the right lawyer isn't always easy and I have already discussed how you should go about it. I would add that you should be very suspicious about a lawyer that tells you what to do before you even hire him/her. I've had people say, 'well another lawyer said I should just comply'. 'So did you hire this lawyer', I ask? 'No, I just called him a few minutes ago'. So without being retained and without speaking to anyone from DCPP, this lawyer is dispensing advice? Sounds like trouble to me. It also doesn't sound like any sort of plan. Also avoid listening to lawyers that tell you that there is nothing any lawyer can do for you. I think I have already demonstrated that such thinking is false.

I realize that some of this is repetitive from the previous chapters but I really had to emphasize that hiring the right lawyer as early as impossible is so important, it just cannot be over stated.

So now that you understand that you should hire a lawyer and you found the right one, you want to know what will happen next. That answer is impossible to give since every single case is different. There are sometimes several options at any one time and we have to talk through them to come up with the right solution. Regardless, your lawyer should be guiding you every single step of the way. If you are talking to the case worker, it's because your lawyer told you to. If you are signing something, it's because your lawyer knows that it says and has authorized you to sign it.

The case worker may want you to do a number of things to work towards closing out the case. This may include evaluations, interviews, speaking to the children, signing releases, etc. What throws people off is that DCPP is not limited to the four corners of the referral. Thus, if you are accused of hitting your child and your child is old enough to convince the case worker that you have never hit him/her; it doesn't mean the case will go away. They can and often will turn your entire life upside down in order to find something.

Even though the referral may have nothing to do with mental health issues, they may start counting your medications and/or asking to speak with your doctors. They may also want your medical records. If the referral did not mention drug use and you have no history of abusing substances, they may still ask for a urine test. This is one of the many ways your lawyer can help you. He or she needs to determine what is necessary to close the case out and what should be avoided. I cannot stress enough that the exact strategy is different in every single case.

The time frame for DCPP to make an investigate finding is usually 60 days. Something on the Internet either tells people or gives them the impression that this is some type of deadline that DCPP is facing. It is far from it. I've seen cases that have been opened for many months even with an attorney's involvement. Without an attorney's involvement, I've heard of some cases staying open for years. Thus, don't worry about this 60 day issue. All you need to worry about is following your attorney's advice.

While the case is open, the case worker may interview your child at school. Unfortunately, there is really nothing you can do to prevent this. The law requires schools to comply with DCPP without seeking permission of the parents first. See N.J.S.A. 18A:36-25 and N.J.A.C. 6A-16-11.1. I really don't suggest that you pump your children full of information or tell them what to say. Chances are, this will come out and this could look much worse than the allegations themselves. Don't worry too much about the allegations that came from your child. Without any type of corroboration, the statement of a child doesn't carry much weight. Of course, if your child's statement is so outrageous, it may indicate coaching or some undiagnosed mental health problem. Be sure to discuss those issues with your attorney.

At the end of the case, you will get a close out letter. In fact, it may actually be two letters. The first letter will tell you what the investigation findings were (see next chapter). The second letter will tell you that the case is being closed out and that services will no longer be provided to your family. If you were not successful in closing out your case, you may receive a letter indicating that the case will remain open and that services will be provided.

The goal of even helping clients through DCPP investigations is to make sure that the case never goes to court and is closed out as soon as possible. While your lawyer may get confirmation that the case is being closed prior to receiving the close out letter, the letter itself is evidence that the efforts of your lawyer were successful. As I will detail in the next chapter, the close out letter may indicate that you have been substantiated even though they are not taking you to court. You should discuss this issue with your lawyer right away.

## 6. INVESTIGATIVE FINDINGS

Every time DCPP receives a referral, it must perform an investigation. At the end of that investigation, they will provide you with a letter detailing their investigate findings. Until mid-2013, DCPP had two options: substantiated or unfounded. To put it in laymen's terms, you were either guilty or not guilty. However, the Administrative Code was changed to allow more flexibility by creating four findings instead of just the two. The specific section of the code is as follows:

> 10:129-7.3(c) For each allegation, the Department representative shall make a finding that an allegation is "substantiated," "established," "not established," or "unfounded".
>
> 1. An allegation shall be "substantiated" if the preponderance of the evidence indicates that a child is an "abused or neglected child" as defined in N.J.S.A. 9:6-8.21 and either the investigation indicates the existence of any of the circumstances in N.J.A.C. 10:129-7.4 or substantiation is warranted based on consideration of the aggravating

and mitigating factors listed in N.J.A.C. 10:129-7.5.

2. An allegation shall be "established" if the preponderance of the evidence indicates that a child is an "abused or neglected child" as defined in N.J.S.A. 9:6-8.21, but the act or acts committed or omitted do not warrant a finding of "substantiated" as defined in (c)1 above.

3. An allegation shall be "not established" if there is not a preponderance of the evidence that a child is an abused or neglected child as defined in N.J.S.A. 9:6-8.21, but evidence indicates that the child was harmed or was placed at risk of harm.

4. An allegation shall be "unfounded" if there is not a preponderance of the evidence indicating that a child is an abused or neglected child as defined in N.J.S.A. 9:6-8.21, and the evidence indicates that a child was not harmed or placed at risk of harm.

(d) A finding of either established or substantiated shall constitute a determination by the Department that a child is an abused or neglected child pursuant to N.J.S.A. 9:6-8.21. A finding of either not established or unfounded shall constitute a determination by the Department that a child is not an abused or neglected child pursuant to N.J.S.A. 9:6-8.21.

Pursuant to N.J.A.C. 10:129-7.7 (a), a Department employee shall disclose only substantiated findings for a Child Abuse Record Information (CARI) check. In other words, you will only be put into the abuse and neglect registry otherwise known as the 'Central

Registry'. Likewise, you can only appeal to the OAL a finding of substantiated. (See next chapter)

With this new four tier scheme, the term substantiated takes on new meaning. Pursuant to N.J.A.C. 10:129-7.4(a), the existence of any one or more of the following circumstances shall require a finding of substantiated when the investigation indicates:

> 1. The death or near death of a child as a result of abuse or neglect;
>
> 2. Subjecting a child to sexual activity or exposure to inappropriate sexual activity or materials;
>
> 3. The infliction of injury or creation of a condition requiring a child to be hospitalized or to receive significant medical attention;
>
> 4. Repeated instances of physical abuse committed by the perpetrator against any child;
>
> 5. Failure to take reasonable action to protect a child from sexual abuse or repeated instances of physical abuse under circumstances where the parent or guardian knew or should have known that such abuse was occurring; or
>
> 6. Depriving a child of necessary care which either caused serious harm or created a substantial risk of serious harm.

In addition, N.J.A.C. 10:129-7.5(a) provides a number of factors to be considered in determining a finding of substantiated or established. Specifically it indicates that the Department representative shall consider the aggravating factors below in determining if abuse or neglect should be substantiated or established:

1. Institutional abuse or neglect;

> 2. The perpetrator's failure to comply with court orders or clearly established or agreed-upon conditions designed to ensure the child's safety, such as a child safety plan or case plan;
>
> 3. The tender age, delayed developmental status, or other vulnerability of the child;
>
> 4. Any significant or lasting physical, psychological, or emotional impact on the child;
>
> 5. An attempt to inflict any significant or lasting physical, psychological, or emotional harm on the child;
>
> 6. Evidence suggesting a repetition or pattern of abuse or neglect, including multiple instances in which abuse or neglect was substantiated or established; and
>
> 7. The child's safety requires separation of the child from the perpetrator.

On the other hand, N.J.A.C. 10:129-7.5(b) states that the Department representative shall consider the mitigating factors below in determining if abuse or neglect should be substantiated or established:

1. Remedial actions taken by the alleged perpetrator before the investigation was concluded;

> 2. Extraordinary, situational, or temporary stressors that caused the parent or guardian to act in an uncharacteristic abusive or neglectful manner;
>
> 3. The isolated or aberrational nature of the abuse or neglect; and
>
> 4. The limited, minor, or negligible physical, psychological, or emotional impact of the abuse or neglect on the child.

Because this is so new, it will take time to fully understand how lawyers representing clients facing a finding of substantiated can use these factors to avoid or change such a finding. We have been very successful in preventing substantiated findings, which has resulted in far fewer fact-finding trials for our firm. This not only helps our clients stay off of the Central Registry but it also saves them a ton of money.

This new scheme also allows DCPP to retain more records than they may have otherwise done in the past. I'm not sure how relevant this really is—at least in my cases, it seemed like DCPP rarely removed records on its own when it should have. Nevertheless, only unfounded records will be eligible for removal from their internal records, but there are many exceptions.

N.J.A.C. 10:129-8.2 states:

(a) A Department employee shall expunge a record which consists of an unfounded report, as specified in N.J.A.C. 10:129-7.3(c)4, three years after determining that the report was unfounded, unless one of the exceptions listed in N.J.A.C. 10:129-8.3 exists.

(b) If unfounded, a Department employee shall expunge the entire record, containing the original report and each subsequent unfounded report, three years after the date of the finding associated with the last report, if a subsequent report received during the three years prior to expunction is likewise unfounded, unless one of the exceptions listed in N.J.A.C. 10:129-8.3 exists.

(c) The Department shall limit routine expunction of records to those which consist of unfounded reports, as specified in N.J.A.C. 10:129-7.3(c)4, for which the finding was made on or after the April 7, 1997 enactment of N.J.S.A. 9:6-8.40a.

(d) The Department shall limit the expunction of a record to its computer file only, if the record consists of a report unfounded prior to April 7, 1997.

If you're like me, and you don't have much faith in DCPP actually removing their records on their own, you can request it. Specifically, N.J.A.C. 10:129-8.2(e) states:

(e) An alleged perpetrator may submit a request, in writing, to the Department of Children and Families, Closed Records Liaison, PO Box 717, Trenton, New Jersey 08625-0717, when he or she seeks expunction of a record that consists of a report that was unfounded prior to April 7, 1997. The Department's Closed Records Liaison shall make a determination on each request in accordance with the criteria contained in this subchapter, and shall advise the alleged perpetrator, in writing, as to whether the Department shall expunge or retain the record.

As I indicated, there are a lot of exceptions to the above rule. Pursuant to N.JA.C. 10:129-8.3(a) the Department employee shall retain a record which contains a report unfounded on or after April 7, 1997, when one or more of the following circumstances exist:

> 1. The investigation of the report results in more than one finding, including both an unfounded and a substantiated, established, or not established finding;
>
> 2. The Division provided services to the alleged child victim, a member of his or her family or household, or the alleged perpetrator, and three years have not passed since a service case was closed or provision of services has been concluded;
>
> 3. The State Central Registry receives a subsequent report regarding the alleged child victim, a member of his or her family or household, or the alleged perpetrator, during the three years prior to eligibility for expunction, and the subsequent report is substantiated, established, or not established;
>
> 4. The outcome of a child protection investigation, a criminal investigation or a court proceeding involving the alleged child victim, a member of his or her family or household or the alleged perpetrator is pending;
>
> 5. A court of competent jurisdiction orders the Department to retain the record;
>
> 6. The Commissioner of the Department of Children and Families or designee requests that the Department retain the record;

7. The State Central Registry receives a subsequent report that the Department is investigating. If the subsequent report is unfounded, then the record is evaluated for expunction three years after the investigation is completed;

8. If an allegation is pending or under investigation at the time of expunction review, the record shall be retained for three years after the case is closed, if that allegation is likewise unfounded, or three years from when the service case is closed; or

9. If a service request is pending or under investigation at the time of expunction review, the record is retained until three years after the case is closed, if that allegation is likewise unfounded, or three years from when the service case is closed.

In addition, N.J.A.C. 10:129-8.3(b) states that the Division shall retain the record of any case where the Division provided out-of-home placement-related services, including, but not limited to, Medicaid, board payments, clothing allowance, or Child Placement Review Board review.

I realize that is a lot to navigate through. It seems like the removal of records is the exception rather than the rule but in my opinion, I never had much faith in DCPP removing records on their own anyway. Since these records cannot be shared with anyone anyway, it will likely have no impact on you if the records are not removed. Thus, I wouldn't lose any sleep over DCPP retaining their records. If it ever presents a problem for you, speak to an attorney right away. I'm sure he/she will be able to find ways to deal with it.

## 7. OAL APPEALS

DCPP can bring someone to court for a variety of reasons. While many people who are substantiated go to court, you don't need to be substantiated to have a complaint filed against you, and not everyone who is substantiated will be brought to court. In general, DCPP will not bring you to court if there is no need to force you to do something or if they are not seeking to limit your parental rights. As I previously indicated, you will receive a close out letter(s) that indicates their findings. If you are substantiated, you can appeal it so as to prevent your name from being added to the Central Registry. However, if your case is already in court, the issue will likely be dealt with as part of the DCPP litigation, so there is probably no need to file the appeal. Of course, you can still do so but they will just tell you that you cannot appeal it while the litigation is pending. You should discuss this issue with your lawyer so that you don't lose your appeal rights.

Although we use the term appeal, it's not really an appeal in the traditional sense. Rather, it's a trial. OAL, the Office of

Administrative Law, is different than any court you have probably dealt with. There are three administrative court houses in New Jersey and just about every case proceeds to trial.

The substantiation letter will advise as to how to file the appeal. All it really takes is a letter. In response to that letter, you will receive an acknowledgment that the appeal was received and that you will be contacted further with more instructions. One of the documents that you will receive shortly thereafter is an OAL Hearing Form, which you will be asked to fill out. The form is to be submitted to the Administrative Hearing Unit (or AHU) which will review the form to see if you are 'eligible' for a hearing in the OAL court.

What the AHU is really doing here for the most part is screening cases to determine if they can block you from ever seeing the inside of a court room. Far too many people fill out this form without the assistance of an attorney. Within a short period of time, a DAG will file a motion for summary disposition which is the same thing as a motion for summary judgment. The DAG will use your own words from this form against you and ask the court to deny your appeal without every taking testimony. While I don't have any statistics to point to, I am sure that they are mostly successful in such applications. So in other words, these people tried to appeal only to have their own words be used against them to deny their right to appeal. This is just another example of why you need a knowledgeable attorney to guide you through every step of the process.

Assuming you handled that form the right way, the next step of the case will be a telephone hearing. This hearing just sets dates for discovery and trial. For whatever reason, the DAG will take many months to get you discovery. Depending on the case, your lawyer may want to make a big deal out of this delay. If the case was in a regular court, discovery would be very prompt. For OAL appeals, obtaining discovery feels like it takes forever. After all, it only takes a few minutes to run a file through a copier. If there is still a delay, your lawyer may want to ask the judge to order that the DCPP file be available for inspection right away. This will give your lawyer more time to prepare if necessary.

It could take years to actually get to trial. Because the OAL trial is a bench trial and the rules of evidence are modified, the trials tend to go pretty quickly. Most are handled in one day. Thus, they can be fairly inexpensive relative to other legal matters that go to trial. Unlike Superior court, the ALJ will likely not be interrupted by any other cases. You will likely be the only case there for that judge so there may be next to no waiting time which also helps to speed up the process.

The case will proceed like any other trial. DCPP will put their case on first. Your lawyer will have the right to cross examine all witnesses. At the end of DCPP's case, the DAG will request that various items be moved into evidence. Your lawyer can stipulate to these items or object to them coming in. Again, the evidence rules are very relaxed so most documents may come in. However, your lawyer can and should argue that the court should give them less weight for one reason or another. Then, your lawyer can put on your case if you have one. You can call witnesses and you can testify if you want. However, you are not forced to put on a case. You can then make oral or written summations depending on the judge.

After the record is closed, the Administrative Law Judge or ALJ will file a written opinion. Both sides can then file exceptions to this opinion. The matter is then turned over to the head of the agency that you are appealing. So in this case, the Director of DCPP will determine whether or not to overrule the initial DCPP finding. If you think that is strange, you are not alone. So even though the ALJ ruled against DCPP, the Director is not bound by those findings. However, the Director cannot just decide to disregard every ALJ decision, as that would make the entire process pointless. There are times when the Director upholds the ALJ's decision even though it goes against DCPP but your lawyer really needs to make a good record that the ALJ can really hang his/her hat on. This will make it more difficult for the Director to overrule the ALJ's findings.

If you ultimately lose your OAL appeal, you can file an appeal with the Appellate Division just as you would any other case. If you fail to file that appeal or win that appeal, your name will be placed on the Central Registry. I will not discuss these appeals in this book as there is not peculiar about them. More information on appeals to the Appellate Division is available at www.njcourtsonline.com.

## 8. ORDER TO INVESTIGATE

DCPP can handle your case out of court or they can bring you to court by filing a complaint against you. There is also an intermediate step where they can ask a court to force to you comply with their investigation so that they can figure out how to handle your case. This is called an Order to Investigate. It starts off with the filing of an application before the court just like any other DCPP case. However, instead of them accusing you of abuse and neglect, they are indicating that there is an allegation and in order for them to make a proper investigative finding, they need you to do something that you have apparently refused to do. While not exactly rare, Orders to Investigate are not filed every day. Even worse is that almost no one actually contests them. As a result, this usually turns into a rubber stamp for DCPP and they will get everything they want. While it sounds grim, there is hope.

If you've read the entire book up until this point, I'm sure you realize that your best hope is to hire a good lawyer. Even most DCPP lawyers have not contested an Order to Investigate, so you have to make sure that any lawyer you hire has the right experience. There is almost no case law on this subject which means that these hearing are not being contested and then appealed. If more lawyers actually contested these cases, you'd see more case law. In addition, I often ask public defenders and others who are in DCPP court every single day about what the judge may or may not do with my order to investigate. They often tell me what I already know: no one really fights these cases. These cases should be fought and you should discuss the best court of action with your lawyer.

I'm not going to copy and paste my briefs on this topic in this book but I will say that I have fought these Orders to Investigate and I have won. There are a number of ways to win and I have probably used a different method with almost all of these cases. The exact strategy will depend on the facts and circumstances of the case itself including but not limited to the lawyer's style and the client's risk tolerance.

Sometimes my strategy is based almost entirely on legal argument while in other cases; I focus more on the facts. Because these cases are so rarely litigated, your lawyer has to be very strong to combat a judge that may view this as a big fight over nothing. So what if your client has to do X, Y, Z, what does it matter? How is he/she going to be harmed? Your lawyer needs to shut those arguments down. You have rights and your rights are not measured by whether or not you will suffer harm or not. Of course, DCPP wouldn't want you to do these things if it didn't have the possibility of harming you in the first place but that's not always the best argument to make as it makes you look like you have something to hide (which you probably do).

After the Order to Investigate no matter which way it goes, DCPP can decide to close its case, keep it open for services or to file a complaint against you.

## 9. THE ORDER TO SHOW CAUSE

If DCPP is going to bring you to court, it can file for Care and Supervision (often called care and supe) or Care, Supervision and Custody. When DCPP files for Care and Supervision, you will still have custody of your children. DCPP will be asking you and/or your children to undergo services. These services can include psychological evaluations, substance abuse treatment, parenting skills training and a whole host of other services. If you should do these services and when should do them is a very important issue that must be discussed with your lawyer.

If DCPP is asking for custody of your children, they will have likely removed them already through a Dodd removal. A Dodd removal allows DCPP to remove your children without a court order. They must then come to court promptly for permission to retain custody. Your children may be placed in a foster home unless other placement, such as a relative, can be quickly found.

DCPP cases are very strange in that your enemy (DCPP) who has turned your life upside down must now help you put everything back to normal. Of course, the extent of their help varies from case to case. Regardless, it's the law. When DCPP has taken your children, the process by which you get them back is called reunification. DCPP must make reasonable efforts to either work toward reunification with the parents or guardians or, if reunification cannot be accomplished, DCPP must attempt to find a permanent placement for the child. N.J.S.A. 9:6–8.8(b)(2)-(4). This reasonable efforts standard is also outlined in Title 30. N.J.S.A. 30:4C-11.2; See also N.J. Div. of Youth & Family Serv's v. I.S., 202 N.J. 145 (2010) (construing N.J.S.A. 30:4C-15.1 in identifying 'reasonable efforts' within the context of termination of parental rights determinations).

To bypass the requirement for reasonable efforts to reunification, 'aggravating circumstances' must be found to exist. N.J. Div. of Youth and Family Serv's v. A.R.G., 361 N.J. Super. 46, 76 (App. Div. 2003), aff'd 179 N.J. 264 (2004).

'Aggravated Circumstances' is defined as:

> 1. That the nature of the abuse or neglect must have been so severe or repetitive that to attempt reunification would jeopardize and compromise the safety of the child, and would place the child in a position of an unreasonable risk to be re-abused.
>
> 2. Moreover, any circumstances that increase the severity of the abuse or neglect, or add to its

injurious consequences, equates to "aggravated circumstances."

3. Where the circumstances created by the parent's conduct create an unacceptably high risk to the health, safety and welfare of the child, they are "aggravated" to the extent that [DYFS] may bypass reasonable efforts of reunification.

4. Where the parental conduct is particularly heinous or abhorrent to society, involving savage, brutal, or repetitive beatings, torture, or sexual abuse, the conduct may also be said to constitute "aggravated circumstances".

Regardless of what DCPP is seeking, most of the first steps will be the same. Keep in mind that you will not receive a formal court notice and in fact, you may not receive anything telling you to go to court. The case worker will often just tell you when to go to court. When you get there, you will be served with a copy of the complaint. As I indicated previously, you will probably freak out when you read it because of all the lies that it contains. No matter how much I warn my clients about this, I just expect it at this point. If you didn't bring your own lawyer, you will be given a public defender on a provisional basis. If you want the public defender's office to represent you, you will have to fill out a form called a 5A.

The court will then determine if you are indigent enough so that you cannot afford your own lawyer.

Once you have your lawyer situation straightened out and you have read the complaint, there are two important decisions to make. The first is whether or not you will go forward with a contested hearing. You have the right to force DCPP to put on its case worker and have him/her testify to the complaint. The other lawyers in the case can then cross examine the case worker. After that, the other lawyers can then put on their own witnesses. So this is basically a mini-trial. However, the standard that DCPP must meet at this point is ridiculously low so it can be nearly impossible to win a contested hearing on the facts. When these cases are contested, you are more likely to win the legal argument over the factual argument.

Of course, there are exceptions to every rule. While it doesn't happen often, there are cases where we have made factual and/or legal arguments at the first court appearance and as a result, the case was thrown out. In fact, we had one case where the entire case was thrown out of court in an hour. This is clear evidence that lawyers who take a one size fits all approach do not know what they are doing.

Instead of having a contested hearing in most of our cases, we often work out a settlement with DCPP whereby we will not have a prolonged contested hearing and we will instead focus on how to move the case forward. How can we get the children back home?

How can we get the client more parenting time? What services can we do right away? How can we close the case ASAP? Answering these questions at the first court appearance are the building blocks of a good strategy to fight back against DCPP and win.

One of the best ways to win a case is to limit, if not eliminate, the arguments between you and your adversary. This is not to say that I am a defeatist or that I just go belly up. Far from it. While I love a good trial just like you see on TV, such court room battles are the exception, not the rule. I win the vast majority of my cases via strategic negotiation. Again, I have to emphasize that this should not be a bad word. There are ways to negotiate a case to get the result you want without really giving up much of anything. Even better still, avoiding protracted legal battles can save you a ton of money.

Unfortunately, too many lawyers go into the Order to Show Cause with absolutely no plan. They treat it as just a procedural step in the case and that everything else can just be dealt with on another day. These are the same lawyers that always tell their clients to refuse all services. Your lawyer may not be able to map out a strategy for the entire case since there is a lot of unknown information at this early stage, but a basic strategy should at least be determined at this point. What is the plan in the case? What will you do? What will you not do? How will these actions help us win the case? If your lawyer doesn't explain all of this to you, he or she is not giving you proper legal advice. I tell my clients what I think they should do and why they should do it. They understand the options and my advice. I then let them call the shots, which is almost always to go along with my suggestion.

At the end of this court date and all other court dates, you will receive a court order. This is the legal document that the judge signed. It says who should be doing what as well as when you will be returning to court. These court orders are very important. You should keep them in a safe place and make sure you understand what is expected of you at all times. Too many people lose their orders and forget what they are supposed to do or when the next court date is. Others don't understand them. If you are confused by something in the order, make your lawyer explain it to you. You can't win a case if you don't know what you are supposed to do and why.

## 10. COMPLIANCE AND CASE MANAGEMENT

The next date after the Order to Show Cause is the Return on the Order to Show Cause. In 99% of cases, it's pretty much a compliance review hearing and/or case management conference, which is what almost all of your court tes will be except for the fact-finding hearing and the permanency hearing. Depending on the judge or the case, compliance hearings may also be called case management conferences, especially if there are no real compliance issues to discuss.

Regardless of what it is called, the court dates are basically the same. In almost all counties, DCPP will provide a court report to the court and all parties in advance of the court date so that everyone is updated on what has happened since the last court date. However, this generally does not occur on the Return on the Order to Show Cause, especially since it takes place so soon after the Order to Show Cause itself. The court report is a very important document, and your lawyer should object to anything that is false, misleading or out dated. In addition, your lawyer should send in his/her own letter to add any facts the court report may have left out.

There are a few counties where DCPP does not provide a court report. In these cases, your lawyer should be updating the court as to your compliance via letter. The letter should summarize the allegations, the services requested and the status of the services. Your lawyer can also remind the court as to the current parenting time arrangement along with any requests to increase the parenting time. Positive collaterals from service providers should also be provided when possible.

Once you get to court, the DAG will update the court further. The Law Guardian will also update the court but in most cases, this update consists of 'I met with the children and they are doing fine in their placement'. The lawyers for the parents can then update the judge on how the clients are doing. In addition, they can make requests of the other parties or the court, make legal arguments and ask questions about any number of issues. It's a pretty open forum and your lawyer should take advantage of that. You should know going into the hearing what your lawyer seeks to accomplish. In some cases, the only thing to accomplish is to just get a new date. A waste of time, I know. However, in other cases, there is much more to accomplish such as getting discovery, setting up services or asking for increased parenting time. Your lawyer should at least make an attempt to work towards ending the case at every court appearance.

I often tell my clients that a DCPP case is like a marathon. You have to keep up running it if you want to win it. In those cases where your parenting time is limited, your best way to get your parenting time back is to keep running the marathon. In many cases, you do that by completing services and getting increased parenting time at as many court dates as possible. It can be a slow and agonizing process even with the best lawyer by your side.

Of course, there are other cases where the strategy calls for you to do no services because you will get your parenting time back by winning the fact-finding hearing or getting the case itself, dismissed. Regardless of what the strategy is, there at least needs to be a strategy. As I previously indicated, every court appearance should be viewed as an opportunity to get closer to winning the case. If that is not done, then there is no real strategy in the first place.

## 11. FACT-FINDING HEARING

At around the six month mark, the court must hold a fact-finding hearing to determine whether the child was abused or neglected within the definition of N.J.S.A. 9:6-8.21(c). So unlike almost all other cases where the trial concludes the case, the fact-finding hearing generally marks only the middle of a DCPP case. The case law indicates that the purpose of a fact-finding hearing, as with all other proceedings under Title Nine, is 'to provide for the protection of children under 18 years of age who have had serious injury inflicted upon them by other than accidental means'. G.S. v. Dep't. of Human Servs., 157 N.J. 161, 171 (1999) (quoting N.J.S.A. 9:6-8.8). The Division must establish at a fact-finding hearing, by a preponderance of the evidence, that the child was abused or neglected and only competent, material and relevant evidence may be admitted. New Jersey Div. of Youth and Family Services v. J.Y., 352 N.J. Super. 245, 262 (App. Div. 2002); New

Jersey Div. of Youth and Family Services v. H.B., 375 N.J. Super. 148, 175 (App. Div. 2005).

This is important because the defendants have fewer rights than they would in other proceedings, such as a criminal trial. The burden of proof is lower and the rules of evidence are relaxed. However, that doesn't mean that the rules of evidence get thrown out the window. Standard objections should still be made at every opportunity. Some judges require the lawyers to submit all objections ahead of time. This helps make the trial go quicker. I've had 20 minute trials drag out for 3 hours while we dealt with evidence issues. Some trials can be as quick as 20 minutes while others can go on for days, even with these evidence issues out of the way.

Prior to the new investigate findings in 2013, the Division was left to either find the defendants substantiated or not substantiated. There was little room for settlement. With the new four tier scheme, we are seeing less fact-finding hearings. Not only can we negotiate a case from substantiated to established, but the Division can actually use one of the other three findings instead of substantiated from the start. Of course, there may be times where defense counsel opts for a fact-finding trial even though the defendant is established but this will likely be rare. Avoiding a fact-finding trial not only saves everyone a lot of time, but it saves the defendants a lot of money.

Most defendants are shocked to learn that the fact-finding hearing may have very little impact on the ultimate outcome of the case. In some cases, the fact-finding hearing will determine the direction of the entire case. In others, it is merely a procedural issue. If the allegation is neglect, such as leaving a child home alone, the defendants may need little to no services. Parenting time may never be impacted. The fact-finding hearing will simply determine whether or not the parent will be placed on the registry. If the allegation is an unexplained injury, the accused parent may have little to no parenting time. If the fact-finding hearing shows that the Division could not prove that this really was abuse, the parent may be quickly reunited with the child. Only your attorney can advise you on the importance of the fact-finding hearing and whether you should go forward.

If the Division will not move off the finding of substantiated, the parents do not have to go to trial. They have the option to stipulate, the DCPP analog of pleading guilty. Lawyers disagree as to whether there is any benefit to stipulating. I think it comes down to money, time, evidence and other possible benefits. If the evidence against the parent is very strong, there is little upside in wasting time and money fighting a losing battle. Stipulating may allow the parent to admit to a better set of facts than what would have come out at trial. For example, if the parent used drugs, passed out, and the child was injured as a result, the parent may be able to say that he/she used drugs and as a result, the child was placed at risk of harm and not that they passed out and/or that the child was actually harmed as a result. While the difference may seem subtle, it could be very helpful considering the alternative.

If the parent does decide to move forward with the fact-finding hearing, the Division will go first as they have the burden of proof. They may call case workers, police officers, school officials, doctors, experts and other witnesses. After the DAG questions a witness, the Law Guardian will cross examine the witness. Then the attorney for the defendants can cross examine the witness as well. This process continues until the Division rests. At various points during the trial, the DAG may mark various items of evidence. This is called marking for identification. In other words, this identifies the item that the witness is referring to. For example, if a case worker was referring to a report, the DAG would have had it marked as P1 (or some other designation). However, it is not yet evidence.

At the end of the Division's case (although it could happen at any time during the Division's case) the DAG will ask to move various exhibits into evidence. The evidence that the Division can use may include 'any writing, record or photograph . . . made as a memorandum or record of any condition, act, transaction, occurrence or event relating to a child in an abuse or neglect proceeding of any hospital or any other public of private institution or agency', provided it meets certain admissibility requirements akin to the business record exception. N.J.S.A. 9:6-8.46(a)(3); see

M.C. III 201 N.J. 346-347. DYFS is permitted to submit into evidence pursuant to N.J.R.E. 803(c) and 801(d), reports by staff personnel or professional consultants. Pursuant to court Rule, "conclusions drawn from the facts stated therein shall be treated as prima facie evidence, subject to rebuttal." R. 5:12-4(d)

The other attorneys can object to either the entire item being entered or part of the item. Common objections are relevance and hearsay, but remember, the evidence rules are relaxed. Despite that, I would still argue that hearsay contained in DCPP reports and other documents should not be considered because it violates the defendant's right to confrontation. Relevance is a very general objection, and most evidence is relevant in some way or another.

Another objection is to make it very specific and shift the focus to prejudice such as 404(b) type evidence. For example, if the allegation is that the parents engaged in domestic violence in front of the children, reports about possible but unproven drug use would be prejudicial and should be kept out. Likewise, prior unfounded DCPP allegations should be objected to.

There may be some documents that contain a mix of admissible and inadmissible evidence. For example, a case worker's report that indicates what the parent said may also have hearsay from third parties who did not testify. This report can be formally redacted by the attorneys or the court can just indicate that it will not consider that hearsay.

## If abuse is substantiated

After the fact-finding hearing, the next step in the case is called the dispositional hearing. While this sounds rather formal, in practice, it rarely ever is. Chances are, this issue has already been worked out. Under N.J.S.A. 9:6-8.51, there are six possible conclusions that the court may come to:

1. Suspended judgment,

2. Return of the child to the parent(s) with possible continued intervention by the Division,

3. Initial placement of the child for 12 months, with the possibility of extending the placement by one year at a time upon proper hearing,

4. Return of the child to parent(s) with an order of protection to outline proper care and behavior by parents,

5. Placement of the parent on probation, and

6. Order mandating "therapeutic services."

N.J.S.A. 9:6-8.51 - N.J.S.A. 9:6-8.58.

The case law indicates the following: A dispositional hearing is used to decide what will ultimately be done with the child. The pivotal question in a dispositional hearing is whether the child will be safe going forward if returned to the parents, and if not, what the proper disposition should be. N.J. Div. of Youth & Family Serv's v. G.M., 198 N.J. 382 (2009). The focus in a dispositional hearing should not be on the child's wishes, but on the child's safety going forward. N.J. Div. of Youth & Family Serv's v. M.D., 417 N.J.Super. 583 (App.Div. 2011).

But again, in most cases, the placement of the child, parenting time and reunification are already being worked on prior to the fact-finding hearing. So at least in my cases, the result of same rarely impacts these issues.

**If abuse is not substantiated**

In N.J. Div. of Youth & Family Servs. v. I.S., 214 N.J. 8, 40-42, cert. denied, 134 S. Ct. 529, (2013), the Supreme Court addressed the interplay between Title Nine actions and Title Thirty actions. The court confirmed that even if the Division cannot prove abuse or neglect under Title Nine, the Family Part still has jurisdiction under Title Thirty to address the parent's need for services and the child's need for protection. Id. At 33. In other words, winning the fact-finding hearing will not always close the case. The court can and often will order services to continue.

## 12. PERMANENCY HEARING

If the case continues after the fact-finding hearing, the rest of the court appearances will likely be compliance reviews. If the child has remained outside of the home for 12 months, the court will hold a permanency hearing to determine the long-term plan for the child. N.J.S.A. 30:4C-61.2. The purpose of the permanency hearing is to decide whether or not the Division should continue to work toward reunification or if they should work towards another plan such as termination of parental rights.

If you get to this point and you don't have an agreement worked out already, there is a good chance that you will lose the permanency hearing. I say this because if you have a good attorney, he or she should have already worked all this out with the Division. As difficult as they can be sometimes, they do work with me on these permanency hearings in addition to other matters. If reunification is not possible at the moment, the Division will often agree to a three month extension. This allows the parent (or parents) to finish out their services so that reunification can occur.

If the permanency hearing will be litigated, your lawyer must be ready to argue either that the Division did not make reasonable efforts, that the delay in reunification was not your fault or that the delay in reunification was actually part of the process. Let's break these down.

Arguing that the Division did not make reasonable efforts can be tough if the ground work hasn't been laid from day one. That's why I often ask for as many services as possible from the initial court appearance (in those cases where such a request is appropriate). These requests must be followed through for the rest of the litigation. By doing that, you will often prevent a permanency hearing to begin with. There are times when DCPP drags their feet and your lawyer must call them out. In fact, I make sure to use the term reasonable efforts when arguing that the case is being unnecessarily delayed so that I can make a proper record. At the permanency hearing, your lawyer may even want to present transcripts to the court where he/she argued that no reasonable efforts were made as a result of one delay or another.

Arguing that a delay was not the fault of the client is a similar but distinct argument. There are many delays when dealing with the Division's service providers. This is especially troubling when it comes to a psychological evaluation as that will recommend other services. Once this evaluation is ordered by the court, it could take several weeks to months to get scheduled. The actual report can then take over a month to be released. If the next court appearance is a month or two after that, there could be four months or more before the court orders more services. Of course, if your attorney is on top of things, all of these delays can be minimized. However, if these repeated delays cannot be avoided, the parent(s) will have an excellent argument to get a three month extension at the permanency hearing.

The other argument to make is that the delay in reunification was part of the natural process. The best scenario for this is substance abuse addiction where there was a relapse a few months into the case. The research and case law makes it clear that relapse is part of recovery. I've had many clients relapse and we didn't even have to worry about the permanency hearing. Of course, timing is everything. If you are going to screw up, doing that early in the case is much better than late in the game. Regardless, your attorney needs to be prepared to argue that one speed bump should not derail the entire case and that a three month extension is appropriate.

If you lose the permanency hearing, it does not mean that the world is over. The Division will continue to offer services and the parents should continue to work towards reunification. I have seen many clients go from the brink of termination of parental rights to reunification. It is possible and you should never lose hope.

## 13. GM HEARINGS

In some cases, the child at issue is taken from one parent and given to the other. At the end of the case, one parent will want the child back while the other will want to retain custody. As a result, a G.M. Hearing will be held to determine where the child should be placed. You can think of a G.M. hearing as custody trial that will usually conclude such a DCPP case. To better understand G.M. hearings, you should understand the case itself.

In N.J. Div. of Youth & Family Servs. v. G.M., 198 N.J. 382 (2009), following a dispute between thirteen-year-old Kadina and her mother, Gloria, Kadina and her eleven-year-old brother Curtis were removed on an emergent basis from the mother's custody in New Jersey. Id. at 388-89 (2009). Following an emergency hearing, the trial judge found potential abuse or neglect as the result of the mother's consumption of alcohol, and he awarded legal custody of the children to DYFS and physical custody to children's father, who lived in Florida. The mother was ordered to undergo a substance abuse evaluation and was permitted reasonable visitation. Id. at 389. Thereafter, a fact-finding hearing was held, but the litigation was terminated before a dispositional hearing took place. Id. at 391-93. Further, before the litigation was terminated, the mother was led to believe that custody of the children would be returned to her. Id. at 392. On the day that the case was terminated, DYFS reversed its position and, in accordance with the children's alleged wishes, sought retention of custody by the father. Id. at 393. The mother was not given the opportunity to meet this new position, but instead, following a proceeding in which no testimony was taken, no documents were introduced into evidence, and no fact-finding was undertaken, the court ordered that the parents share joint legal custody of the two children, with the father being the primary custodial parent and the mother receiving parenting time. Any change in custody was ordered to proceed through the matrimonial docket. Ibid.

In response, the New Jersey Supreme court stated that "the statutory framework of Title Nine provides that upon a finding of abuse and neglect, the offending parent or guardian is entitled to a dispositional hearing to determine whether the children may safely return to his or her custody, and if not, what the proper disposition should be." Id. at 387-88.

In a dispositional hearing, the court must hear evidence to determine "whether the children may safely be released to the custody of [the parent against whom the FN case was brought] . . . or whether . . . some other disposition is appropriate." Id. at 402; see also N.J.S.A. 9:6-8.51. A dispositional hearing is defined as one that determines "what order should be made" in the litigation. N.J.S.A. 9:6-8.45. Once the trial court decides whether the Division has sustained its allegations of abuse and neglect in a fact-finding hearing, a dispositional hearing immediately follows, N.J.S.A. 9:6-8.47(a), and steers the appropriate course of the case. N.J.S.A. 9:6-8.50. N.J.S.A. 9:6-8.51(a) sets out a menu of dispositions available to the judge.

The dispositional hearing is a critical stage in Title Nine proceedings and must be conducted "'with scrupulous adherence to procedural safeguards,'" with the trial court's conclusions based on material and relevant evidence. G.M., supra, 198 N.J. at 401 (citing N.J. Div. of Youth & Family Servs. v. A.R.G., 179 N.J. 264, 286 (2004)); N.J.S.A. 9:6-8.46(b), (c)). "[T]he central question in a Title 9 dispositional hearing is whether the child may be safely returned to the custody of the parent from whom the child was removed." N.J. Div. of Youth & Family Servs. v. N.D., 417 N.J. Super. 96 (App. Div. 2010) (citing N.J. Div. of Youth & Family Servs. v. G.M., 198 N.J. 382 , 401-05 (2009)).

Thus, if you are facing a G.M. hearing, you need to make sure your lawyer is fully prepared for a custody hearing where the focus will be on why the child should be returned to you or why the child should remain with you, depending on which side of the case you are on. If you are the parent that lost the child, your goal should be to get the child back even before the fact-finding hearing if possible. This can help you avoid a fact-finding hearing. Keep in mind that the longer the child stays away from you, the easier it is to keep the child there.

## 14. FG COMPLAINTS

After losing the permanency hearing, DCPP will file a complaint for guardianship. This is called an FG complaint. In most cases, DCPP will be looking to terminate your parental rights although they do have other options such as Kinship Legal Guardianship. FG cases may start out a little slow at first, which is good because you need as much time as possible. While DCPP has changed their goal, they still have to keep reunification as a concurrent goal in most cases. Thus, the first few court appearances may seem exactly the same as the FN case where you just have one compliance review after another.

Perfection is almost 100% required at this point in the case as there is no time left to make mistakes. Almost all of my clients who I represented at the beginning of the FN case have been able to avoid an FG case. However, we have been hired to represent people at the start of the FG case. Talk about walking into a mess.

We have been able to come into a case where a client had almost no parenting time and then work very hard to get the FG complaint dismissed. It takes time to put a termination of parental rights trial together (otherwise known as a TPR trial) and if perfect compliance can be achieved during this time, a good lawyer can make a lot of progress during each court appearance. Eventually, there is so much progress that DCPP may realize that it is going to be very difficult to win a TPR trial at that point given the relationship between parent and child that has been at least partially restored. Thus, DCPP can dismiss the FG case and reactivate the FN case. If this is not successful, then you will have to go through with the TPR trial.

The exact defense against the FG complaint will depend on why you got there in the first place and what DCPP is seeking (i.e. KLG versus TPR). If it is a matter of compliance, you must achieve perfection as I have previously indicated. You also really need to push for increasing visitation at every opportunity. Thus, you have to be careful of large gaps of times in between each court appearance. If it seems like you are actually going to proceed with a TPR or KLG trial, you'll have to gear up for the fight of your life.

## 15. TERMINATION OF PARENTAL RIGHTS

Before I discuss strategy, let's understand the law first. If a child has been put in placement, filing for termination of parental rights must commence before that child has spent 15 of the last 22 months in placement or whenever any of the five standards set forth in the statute are satisfied. N.J.S.A. 30:4C–15.1. Filing for termination of parental rights is not required under the three exceptions outlined in N.J.S.A. 30:4C-15.3, which require that (1) the child is placed with a relative and a permanent plan can be achieved without termination of parental rights, (2) the Division has documented compelling reasons why terminating parental rights would not be in the best interests of the child, or (3) the Division was required to provide reasonable efforts to reunify the family but has not yet provided the services that would facilitate a safe return home for the child.

The State, as parens patriae, may sever the parent-child relationship to protect the child from serious physical and emotional injury. W.P. and M.P., supra, 308 N.J. Super. at 382. When the child's biological parent resists termination of parental rights, it is the court's function to decide whether the parent can raise the child without causing harm. J.C., supra, 129 N.J. at 10. The cornerstone of the inquiry is not whether the parent is fit, but whether the parent can become fit to assume the parental role within time to meet the child's needs. Ibid. (citing A.W., supra, 103 N.J. at 607). "The analysis . . . entails strict standards to protect the statutory and constitutional rights of the natural parents." J.C., supra, 129 N.J. at 10. "The burden rests on the party seeking to terminate parental rights 'to demonstrate by clear and convincing evidence' that the risk of 'serious and lasting [future] harm to the child' is sufficiently great as to require severance of the parental ties" W.P. & M.P., supra, 308 N.J. Super. at 383 (quoting J.C., supra, 129 N.J. at 10).

The question for the court "focuses upon what course serves the 'best interests' of the child." W.P. & M.P., supra, 308 N.J. Super. at 383. The State Constitution and N.J.S.A. 30:4C-15 and 15.1a require satisfaction of the "best interests of the child" test by clear and convincing evidence before termination of parental rights can occur. See A.W., supra, 103 N.J. at 612; In re Guardianship of Jordan, supra, 336 N.J. Super. at 274. Specifically, the four-prong test set forth in N.J.S.A. 30:4C-15.1a requires the Division to prove:

> (1) The child's safety, health or development has been or will continue to be endangered by the parental relationship;

(2) The parent is unwilling or unable to eliminate the harm facing the child or is unable or unwilling to provide a safe and stable home for the child and the delay of permanent placement will add to the harm. Such harm may include evidence that separating the child from his resource family [formerly referred to as "foster"] parents would cause serious and enduring emotional or psychological harm to the child;

(3) The [D]ivision has made reasonable efforts to provide services to help the parent correct the circumstances which led to the child's placement outside the home and the court has considered alternatives to termination of parental rights; and

(4) Termination of parental rights will not do more harm than good.

These standards are neither discrete nor separate. In re Guardianship of K.H.O., 161 N.J. 337, 348 (1999). They overlap to provide a composite picture of what may be necessary to advance the best interests of the children. Ibid. "The considerations involved in determinations of parental fitness are 'extremely fact sensitive' and require particularized evidence that address the specific circumstances in the given case." Ibid. (quoting In re Adoption of Children by L.A.S., 134 N.J. 127, 139 (1993)).

The standard set forth in N.J.S.A. 30:4C-15.1 is known as the 'best interests of the child' test and it sets forth the central questions in termination of parental rights proceedings. Termination of parental rights should always be decided based on the child's wellness, whether it is because it is in the child's best interest to terminate parental rights, or the family has failed to – despite reasonable efforts by the Division – eliminate the circumstances that led to the initial placement. N.J.S.A. 30:4C-15.1. That statute defines "reasonable efforts" as "attempts by an agency authorized by the division to assist the parents in remedying the circumstances and conditions that led to the placement of the child and in reinforcing the family structure". For the most part, this means services.

TPR trials for my firm are rare. First, most of my clients avoid the FG filing all together because we are able to set up winning strategies to defeat the FN case. Those that hire us for FG cases have almost always been able to avoid a TPR trial. A TPR trial is rather complicated and it often involves a number of experts. Since each side may have their own experts, this is what we often call a battle of experts. Careful thought must go into a TPR trial. It will take everything your lawyer has to win, and like everything else, there is no one way to win.

If I am faced with a TPR trial and no way to avoid it, I would first comb through every document in the file and listen back to every court appearance. Any and all methods to attack DCPP's lack of reasonable efforts should be demonstrated. It would then be helpful if this summary with exhibits is provided to your expert to be incorporated into his/her report. I assume that you will have an expert as it is can be difficult to impossible to do a trial without one. However, I seriously doubt that many TPR trials go forward without an expert anyway as I can't see the court even allowing this to occur as it would leave the natural parent almost defenseless.

Your lawyer should also pull up as many Appellate Division cases that are similar in one way to another to your case. There are a ton of unreported cases involving TPR trials and while most are bad, some have been reversed. Even if the cases are not in your favor, they will provide insight into how other people have lost and what mistakes your lawyer can avoid.

I sincerely hope that you will never have to actually face a TPR trial.

## 16. KINSHIP-LEGAL GUARDIANSHIP

Kinship-legal guardianship ("KLG") is an alternative to termination of parental rights. It allows the natural parents to maintain a relationship with their children and may even permit reunification in the future. This is only a good alternative when TPR seems likely. It should be avoided at all costs while reunification is pursued.

KLG leaves the door cracked open for the parents to someday regain custody. However, I question how often this actually occurs. Children tend to grow roots; that is, once they settle into a particular place, it can be very hard to move them. Likewise, the adults assuming the guardianship role over the children tend to get attached to them as well. You'd be amazed how many relatives fight the natural parents to hold onto their children.

Whether the case is appropriate for TPR or KLG should be discussed at the permanency hearing. However, I have had some cases where a determination as to whether or not KLG was appropriate could not be made until months after the permanency hearing. If a permanency hearing in your case is even scheduled, you need to get on the same page with DCPP as much as possible. What is their plan for permanency? Has KLG been ruled out? If so, why? What can your lawyer do about that to make KLG a possibility?

To help you understand what KLG is, I will go through some of the relevant case law on the issue. Kinship legal guardianship exists as an alternate vehicle to termination of parental rights where 'adoption of the child is neither feasible nor likely'. P.P., supra, 180 N.J. 494, 509. It is designed as another way to promote the State's strongly held public policy to foster the 'essential and overriding interest' all children have 'in stability and permanency', In re Guardianship of J.C., 129 N.J. 1, 26 (1992), i.e., 'as much permanency as possible', P.P., supra, 180 N.J. at 510, notwithstanding that adoption will not occur.

Such a guardianship is clearly intended to formalize the status of a relative who agrees to take on responsibility for a child, *see* N.J.S.A. 3B:12A-4a(1), and can remain in place throughout the child's minority, N.J.S.A. 3B:12A-4a(6). Unlike a judgment terminating parental rights, kinship legal guardianship would not cut off the legal relationship of the parent and child. N.J.S.A. 3B:12A-4a(2) [to] (5).That is, the parent remains entitled to visitation and responsible for child support; [the parent] also has the right to seek termination of the guardianship and a resumption of custody if at a later date [ ]he is able to provide a safe and secure home for the child. Division of Youth and Family Servs. v. S.V., 362 N.J.Super. 76, 87 (App. Div.(2003) (quoted in P.P., supra, 180 N.J. at 510).]

While my firm has litigated KLG trials, I don't think that too many actually get litigated (compared to TPR trials). As a corollary to termination of parental rights, KLG, because of its profound, if not necessarily permanent, effects on the parent-child relationship, requires application of the high 'clear and convincing' standard of proof, as well as other safeguards. Thus, the requirements of the KLG Act to an extent mirror those set forth in the best interests standard of N.J.S.A. 30:4C–15.1, applicable in a termination of parental rights context. Because of this close correspondence between the two statutes; precedent applicable in a termination context is also applicable to KLG cases. Div. of Youth & Family Servs. v. S.F., 392 N.J. Super. 201, 212 n. 5 (App.Div.), certif. denied, 192 N.J. 293 (2007). Nonetheless, the first prong of N.J.S.A. 3B:12A–6d differs from the first prong of N.J.S.A. 30:4C–15.1, which provides that termination shall be granted upon clear and convincing evidence, among other things, that "(1) The child's safety, health or development has been or will continue to be endangered by the parental relationship".

As with termination of parental rights, if KLG is an option, you must discuss with your attorney the best route to take for your case. If DCPP is fighting against a KLG, sometimes the issue hanging is whether the caregiver is appropriate.

Although kinship legal guardians are typically relatives of the child at issue, the statute does not require a biological relationship to exist. See N.J.S.A. 3B:12A-2 (defining "Caregiver" to include a resource family parent or "foster" parent and defining "Kinship legal guardian" to be "a caregiver who is willing to assume care of a child due to parental incapacity, with the intent to raise the child to adulthood, and who is appointed the kinship legal guardian of the child by the court . . ."). In making a determination to appoint a person as a kinship legal guardian, the judge is directed to consider twelve criteria set forth in N.J.S.A. 3B:12A–6a. Your lawyer will need to remind DCPP of this because I have heard DAGs say that the caregiver is not an appropriate KLG because they are not a relative.

So far, we've established what a KLG is, gone through the standard to determine if KLG is appropriate and then discussed whether a caregiver is an appropriate guardian. Assuming all of that has been accomplished by DCPP, we need to discuss what the caregiver's rights are as a KLG. A KLG imposes many of the same rights and responsibilities on the guardian as a custody order places on the custodial parent. Those rights and responsibilities are found in N.J.S.A. 3B:12A–4a, which states:

> [the] guardian shall have the same rights, responsibilities and authority relating to the child as a birth parent, including, but not limited to: making decisions concerning the child's care and well-being; consenting to routine and emergency medical and mental health needs; arranging and consenting to educational plans for the child; ...

responsibility for activities necessary to ensure the child's safety, permanency and well-being; and ensuring the maintenance and protection of the child.

Just like a non-custodial parent in a custody case, in a KLG case, the birth parents must pay child support (if requested by the guardians), N.J.S.A. 3B:12A–4a(3). However, they do enjoy the right to visitation with the child. N.J.S.A. 3B:12A–4a(4).

As I previously mentioned, KLG leaves the door open for the natural parent to regain custody. This is done by filing a motion just as one would file a motion to change custody. Although N.J.S.A. 3B:12A–6(f) does not indicate which party has the burden of proof to show that a KLG order should be vacated, the case law indicates that the burden falls on the moving party. The statute requires a showing that the circumstances that led to the KLG order have changed so "that the parental incapacity or inability to care for the child that led to the original award of [KLG] is no longer the case." Ibid. In other words, a showing of changed circumstances is necessary before a KLG order can be modified. This is the same standard applied for modifying a child custody order, where the burden is on the party seeking to modify the order to demonstrate changed circumstances and that the order is no longer in the child's best interests. Abouzahr v. Matera–Abouzahr, 361 N.J.Super. 135, 152 (App.Div.), certif. denied, 178 N.J. 34 (2003); see also Lepis v. Lepis, 83 N.J. 139, 157 (1980) (party seeking modification of child support has the burden of showing 'changed circumstances' and that such modification is in the child's best interests).

In many cases, these motions can be close to pointless. Unless the natural parent can demonstrate that the KLG is unfit, I don't think you will see too many natural parents winning these motions if the KLG fights back. Instead, the better course of action is to find a KLG that is willing to give the child back at some point if that is permissible. Thus, if DCPP fights the request, the KLG can actually join in on the motion. That is the only way that I see this aspect of KLG having any real applicability.

# CONCLUSION

I hope that you found this book helpful. Please do not hesitate to reach you to me with any comments, questions or suggestions. If you find yourself in a tough DCPP case and you don't have the ability to hire a good lawyer, just remember to fight as hard as you can but you also need to fight smart. Don't let your emotions get the best of you. Getting mad at the case worker, the judge or anyone else will not solve your problems. No matter how bad things look, never give up. Having the right attitude is very important. You need to be honest with yourself and acknowledge any of your faults and work to improve them. You also need to realize that some of this is to an extent a game. The better you play the game, the faster it will all be over. I truly wish you and your family the best of luck.

CPSIA information can be obtained
at www.ICGtesting.com
Printed in the USA
BVHW042134090919
558016BV00007B/109/P